POCKET MANAGEMENT STANDARDS

Management

Level 3

D1331515

MCI, Russell Square House, 10-12 Russell Square, London WC1B 5BZ
Telephone 0171 872 9000
Website http://www.bbi.co.uk/mci
e-mail nfmed_mci@compuserve.com
Registered Charity No. 1002554

Management Charter Initiative is the operating arm of the National
Forum for Management Education and Development.

The National Occupational Standard for Management was developed by MCI with funding from
the Department for Education and Employment.

First published 1998

ISBN 1 897587 75 9

Text processing and typesetting by Digital Type
Printed and bound in Great Britain by Cambridge University Press

Contents

Introduction   1

Management Standards

    Mandatory Units

    Unit A1 Maintain activities to meet requirements   6

    Unit B1 Support the efficient use of resources   14

    Unit C1 Manage yourself   20

    Unit C4 Create effective working relationships   26

    Unit D1 Manage information for action   34

    Optional Units

    Unit C7 Contribute to the selection of personnel for activities   44

    Unit C9 Contribute to the development of teams and
individuals   50

    Unit C12 Lead the work of teams and individuals to achieve
their objectives   60

    Unit C15 Respond to poor performance in your team   68

    Unit E5 Identify improvements to energy efficiency   74

    Unit E8 Provide advice and support for improving
energy efficiency   80

    Unit F5 Provide advice and support for the development
and implementation of quality systems   88

    Unit F7 Carry out quality audits   98

Index   105

Acknowledgements

MCI gratefully acknowledges the assistance of over 4,000 managers and hundreds of employing organisations from all sectors of the economy who participated in the revision and piloting of these standards; the financial support of the Department for Education and Employment; and the Steering Group members, individuals, consultants and MCI staff who have contributed to the development and authorship of this publication.

Management Standards and Qualifications

Developed through consultation with tens of thousands of managers throughout the private, public and voluntary sectors, the Management Standards define benchmarks of best practice in management in the UK today. They describe the standard of performance which is expected of you in the wide variety of functions you carry out as a manager or supervisor.

If you can prove to an assessor that you consistently perform to these *National Standards*, you can be awarded a National Vocational Qualification (NVQ) or Scottish Vocational Qualification (SVQ). NVQs and SVQs in Management are available at the three highest levels, known as levels 3, 4 and 5 (levels 1 and 2 cover technical, administrative and other non-management functions).

This booklet *Management Level 3* covers all the units of the Management Standards at NVQ/SVQ level 3. It is for you if you are a practising manager or supervisor with:

- a defined area of responsibility
- some authority for taking decisions and managing budgets
- responsibility for achieving specific results by using resources effectively
- responsibility for allocating work to team members, colleagues or contractors.

If you are aspiring to become a manager or supervisor, you will find these standards a useful guide to what will be expected of you in your first management position.

Units of Competence

The Management Standards are expressed in a number of *units of competence*, each unit describing a specific management function. The units contain *performance criteria*, clear statements which allow you to assess whether you are performing to the national standard. If you are taking an NVQ or SVQ, your assessor will need to be sure you consistently meet all these criteria in order to certify that you are competent.

The standards specify *knowledge requirements*, what you need to know and understand in order to perform to the national standard. They also identify the *personal competencies*, the skills and attitudes which are essential for effective performance, described as behaviours which it is possible to observe. You can therefore read appropriate management books or attend development programmes to ensure you have the necessary knowledge and skills. If you are unsure about your performance in a particular area, you can use the Management Standards to diagnose the knowledge or skills development you require.

Finally, the standards specify *evidence requirements*. These clearly state the evidence you need to convince your NVQ/SVQ assessor or your line manager that you are competent.

Coverage of Management Level 3

Management Level 3 covers the full range of general management activities which managers working at this level are expected to carry out. It does not, however, cover specialist functions (such as sales, accounting or engineering) which are covered by other, specialist standards.

You will find your work as a manager or supervisor is reflected in the four generic key roles: *A Manage Activities, B Manage Resources, C Manage People* and

Management Standards and Qualifications

D Manage Information. You may also have some specialist responsibilities which are covered in the specialist management key roles of *E Manage Energy* and *F Manage Quality*.

Unit A1 *Maintain activities to meet requirements* is about ensuring the activities for which you are responsible continuously meet the requirements of your organisation and your customers.

Unit B1 *Support the efficient use of resources* covers recommending the resources you and your team need to meet your objectives, and monitoring and controlling the way in which these resources are used.

Unit C1 *Manage yourself* is about developing your own skills and managing your time so that you can meet your objectives.

Unit C4 *Create effective working relationships* is about creating and maintaining effective working relationships with your manager, team members and other colleagues within your organisation.

Unit C7 *Contribute to the selection of personnel for activities* applies to both the internal and external recruitment of people for permanent, temporary or project work. It applies equally to paid or voluntary work, whether full-time or part-time.

Unit C9 *Contribute to the development of teams and individuals* covers helping to identify people's development needs, planning to meet those needs, carrying out development activities and assessing members of your team to see how they have progressed.

Unit C12 *Lead the work of teams and individuals to achieve their objectives*

covers planning and assessing work and providing feedback to team members.

Unit C15 *Respond to poor performance in your team* is about helping to deal with team members whose performance is unsatisfactory. It covers both providing help to deal with problems and contributing to disciplinary and grievance procedures.

Unit D1 *Manage information for action* covers gathering the information you need, providing information and advice to others, and holding meetings.

Units E5 and E8 are specifically about managing energy resources and units F5 and F7 specifically about managing quality.

Gaining a Management NVQ or SVQ

To be assessed for a Management NVQ or SVQ, you must register with an approved centre (details available from MCI). In contrast to academic qualifications, with NVQs and SVQs there is no prescribed course of study. The centre will provide you with advice on any areas where you need to develop new knowledge and skills. The centre itself may offer management development programmes, or it may refer you to other management courses, text books, open and flexible learning schemes or other development activities.

The centre will also provide you with guidance on how to prepare for assessment and allocate you an assessor who will assess your competence. If you are taking and NVQ/SVQ in Management Level 3, you will be assessed against the 5 mandatory units (highlighted in bold on the page opposite) plus any two optional units which you are free to choose.

You will need to gather evidence of your competence which will include products and outcomes of your work activities as well as short reports of your own and statements from others who have observed your performance. You will submit this evidence to your assessor together with your claim for competence. After an assessment interview, your assessor will make one of three credit recommendations: that you are competent, not yet competent, or that you have not provided sufficient evidence to make a decision. If you are assessed as competent, you will be awarded your NVQ or SVQ.

Continuously improving your performance

Your use of the Management Standards does not end with your award of the NVQ or SVQ. When you are familiar with the standards and their performance criteria, it is easy to use them on a daily basis to check that you are working to the benchmarks of best practice. As you take on new tasks and responsibilities, you can prepare to meet these by developing the necessary knowledge and skills which you will find in other specialist standards. If you are given greater authority and autonomy as a manager, you may wish to start looking at higher level Management Standards and preparing for an NVQ or SVQ in Management at level 4.

Management

Level 3

NVQ/SVQ

Mandatory units
Candidates take ALL FIVE mandatory units

Maintain activities to meet requirements

Unit summary

This unit is about ensuring that the activities for which you are responsible meet the requirements of your organisation and your customers. This involves agreeing, planning and monitoring work activities, maintaining suitable work conditions and continuously looking for ways to improve work activities.

This unit contains three elements

A1.1 *Maintain work activities to meet requirements*
A1.2 *Maintain healthy, safe and productive working conditions*
A1.3 *Make recommendations for improvements to work activities.*

Personal competencies

In performing effectively in this unit, you will show that you

Building teams
- keep others informed about plans and progress
- clearly identify what is required of others
- invite others to contribute to planning and organising work

Communicating
- identify the information needs of listeners
- adopt communication styles appropriate to listeners and situations, including selecting an appropriate time and place
- use a variety of media and communication aids to reinforce points and maintain interest

Focusing on results
- maintain a focus on objectives
- tackle problems and take advantage of opportunities as they arise
- actively seek to do things better
- use change as an opportunity for improvement
- monitor quality of work and progress against plans

Thinking and taking decisions
- break processes down into tasks and activities
- identify a range of elements in and perspectives on a situation
- identify implications, consequences or causal relationships in a situation
- take decisions which are realistic for the situation.

Maintain activities to meet requirements

Element A1.1

Maintain work activities to meet requirements

Performance criteria

You must ensure that

a) you agree **requirements** with **customers** in sufficient detail to allow work to be planned

b) you explain **requirements** to **relevant people** in sufficient detail and at an appropriate level and pace

c) you confirm with **relevant people** their understanding of, and commitment to, meeting **requirements**

d) your monitoring of your team's work takes place at appropriate intervals and complies with your organisation's procedures

e) the work under your control normally meets agreed **requirements**

f) when products, services and processes do not meet agreed **requirements**, you take prompt and effective corrective action

g) records relating to the work under your control are complete, accurate and in line with your organisation's procedures

h) you give opportunities to **relevant people** to make recommendations for improving work activities.

Knowledge requirements

You need to know and understand

Communication
- how to communicate effectively with team members, colleagues, line managers and people outside your organisation

Customer relations
- the importance of a focus on customer requirements and quality issues, and your role and responsibilities in relation to this
- the differences between internal and external customers
- how to identify customer requirements to a level of detail sufficient for planning work

Involvement and motivation
- how to encourage and enable team members, colleagues and line managers to help to improve efficiency

Monitoring and evaluation
- how to monitor work activities and take corrective action to ensure requirements are being met

Organisational context
- the records which need to be completed and how this should be done

Planning
- the principles of planning work activities, setting objectives and priorities to ensure requirements are met efficiently.

Evidence requirements

You must prove that you *maintain work activities to meet requirements* to the National Standard of competence.

To do this, you must provide evidence to convince your assessor that you consistently meet **all** the performance criteria.

Your evidence must be the result of real work activities undertaken by yourself. Evidence from simulated activities is **not** acceptable for this element.

You must show evidence that you agree **all** the following types of **requirements**
- quality
- quantity
- delivery
- health and safety.

You must show evidence that you agree requirements with **one** of the following types of **customer**
- internal
- external.

You must also show that you explain work activities and provide opportunities for making recommendations to **one** of the following types of **relevant people**
- team members
- colleagues working at your level
- higher-level managers or sponsors
- people outside your organisation.

You must, however, convince your assessor that you have the necessary knowledge, understanding and skills to be able to perform competently in respect of **all** types of **customer** and **relevant people,** listed above.

Maintain activities to meet requirements

Element A1.2

Maintain healthy, safe and productive working conditions

Performance criteria

You must ensure that

a) you inform **relevant people** about their legal and organisational responsibilities for maintaining healthy, safe and productive **working conditions**

b) you give sufficient support to **relevant people** to ensure they are able to work in a healthy, safe and productive way

c) you give opportunities to **relevant people** to make recommendations for improving **working conditions**

d) **working conditions** under your control conform to organisational and legal requirements

e) **working conditions** under your control are as conducive to the work activity as possible within organisational constraints

f) you respond to breaches in health and safety requirements in ways which are prompt and consistent with organisational and legal requirements

g) you make recommendations for improving **working conditions** clearly and promptly to **relevant people**

h) your records relating to health and safety and **working conditions** are complete, accurate and comply with organisational and legal requirements.

Knowledge requirements

You need to know and understand

Analytical techniques
- how to assess current working conditions and identify possible areas for improvement

Communication
- how to communicate effectively with team members, colleagues, line managers and people outside your organisation

Health and safety
- the importance of health and safety at work and your role and responsibility in relation to this
- the organisational and legal requirements for maintaining a healthy, safe and productive work environment
- the types of support it may be necessary to provide on health and safety issues and how to provide such support
- how to monitor work conditions to ensure they meet health and safety requirements

Organisational context
- how to respond to contradictions between health and safety requirements and organisational demands and constraints
- the procedures to follow in order to recommend improvements in working conditions
- the records which need to be kept and the organisational and legislative requirements for doing so

Workplace organisation
- the types of work conditions which are most conducive to productive work.

Evidence requirements

You must prove that you *maintain healthy, safe and productive working conditions* to the National Standard of competence.

To do this, you must provide evidence to convince your assessor that you consistently meet **all** the performance criteria.

Your evidence must be the result of real work activities undertaken by yourself. Evidence from simulated activities is **not** acceptable for this element.

You must show evidence that you provide information, support and recommendations to **two** of the following types of **relevant people**
- team members
- colleagues working at your level
- higher-level managers or sponsors
- people outside your organisation.

Your evidence must cover **all** the following **working conditions**
- physical environment
- equipment
- materials
- working procedures.

You must, however, convince your assessor that you have the necessary knowledge, understanding and skills to be able to perform competently in respect of **all** types of **relevant people**, listed above.

UNIT A1

Maintain activities to meet requirements

Make recommendations for improvements to work activities

Performance criteria

You must ensure that

a) you provide opportunities for **relevant people** to suggest ways of improving activities

b) your recommendations for improvements to activities are based on sufficient, valid and reliable information

c) your recommendations for improvements are consistent with the objectives of your team and your organisation

d) your recommendations take into account the impact of introducing changes on other parts of your organisation

e) you make recommendations promptly to the **relevant people**

f) you present your recommendations in a manner and form consistent with your organisation's procedures.

Knowledge requirements

You need to know and understand

Analytical techniques
- how to assess current working practices and identify possible areas for improvement
- how to identify the implications of change for other parts of your organisation

Communication
- how to communicate effectively with team members, colleagues, line managers and people outside your organisation
- how to present and argue a case for change most effectively

Continuous improvement
- the importance of continuous improvement in the management of activities and your responsibilities in relation to this

Organisational context
- the procedures to follow in order to recommend improvements in working practices.

Evidence requirements

You must prove that you *make recommendations for improvements to work activities* to the National Standard of competence.

To do this, you must provide evidence to convince your assessor that you consistently meet **all** the performance criteria.

Your evidence must be the result of real work activities undertaken by yourself. Evidence from simulated activities is **not** acceptable for this element.

You must show evidence that you provide opportunities for suggestions and make recommendations to **two** of the following types of **relevant people**
- team members
- colleagues working at the same level
- higher-level managers or sponsors
- specialists.

You must, however, convince your assessor that you have the necessary knowledge, understanding and skills to be able to perform competently in respect of **all** types of **relevant people,** listed above.

Support the efficient use of resources

Unit summary

This unit is about the efficient management of resources for which you have authority and responsibility. It covers recommending the resources you and your team need to meet your objectives. It also covers monitoring and controlling the way in which resources are used.

This unit contains two elements

B1.1 *Make recommendations for the use of resources*
B1.2 *Contribute to the control of resources.*

Personal competencies

In performing effectively in this unit, you will show that you

Communicating

- listen actively, ask questions, clarify points and rephrase others' statements to check mutual understanding
- identify the information needs of listeners
- adopt communication styles appropriate to listeners and situations, including selecting an appropriate time and place

Focusing on results

- maintain a focus on objectives
- tackle problems and take advantage of opportunities as they arise
- prioritise objectives and schedule work to make the best use of time and resources

Thinking and taking decisions

- produce a variety of solutions before taking a decision
- make use of, and reconcile, a variety of perspectives when making sense of a situation
- produce your own ideas from experience and practice
- take decisions which are realistic for the situation.

Support the efficient use of
resources

Element B1.1

Make recommendations for the use of resources

Performance criteria

You must ensure that

a) you give **relevant people** the opportunity to provide information on the resources your team needs

b) your **recommendations** for the use of resources take account of relevant past experience

c) your **recommendations** take account of trends and developments which are likely to affect the use of resources

d) your **recommendations** are consistent with team objectives and organisational policies

e) your **recommendations** clearly indicate the potential benefits you expect from the planned use of resources

f) your **recommendations** are presented to **relevant people** in an appropriate and timely manner.

Knowledge requirements

You need to know and understand

Analytical techniques
- how to analyse the use of resources in the past, and utilise the results to make recommendations on more effective use of resources in the future

Communication
- how to communicate effectively with team members, colleagues and line managers
- how to develop and argue an effective case for changes in the management of resources

Involvement and motivation
- how to enable people to identify and communicate the resources they need

Organisational context
- team objectives and organisational policies regarding the use of resources
- organisational procedures for making recommendations on the use of resources
- the trends and developments which may influence the future use of resources and how to plan for these

Resource management
- the importance of effective management of resources to organisational performance
- the principles underpinning the effective and efficient management of resources
- the importance of keeping accurate records on the use of resources.

Evidence requirements

You must prove that you *make recommendations for the use of resources* to the National Standard of competence.

To do this, you must provide evidence to convince your assessor that you consistently meet **all** the performance criteria.

Your evidence must be the result of real work activities undertaken by yourself. Evidence from simulated activities is **not** acceptable for this element.

You must show evidence that you seek information from, and make recommendations to, at least **two** of the following types of **relevant people**
- team members
- colleagues working at the same level
- higher-level managers or sponsors.

You must also show evidence that you make **both** of the following types of **recommendations**
- short term
- medium term.

You must, however, convince your assessor that you have the necessary knowledge, understanding and skills to be able to perform competently in respect of **all** types of **relevant people**, listed above.

Support the efficient use of
resources

Element B1.2

Contribute to the control of resources

Performance criteria

You must ensure that

a) you give **relevant people** opportunities to take individual responsibility for the efficient use of resources

b) you monitor the use of resources under your control at appropriate intervals

c) the use of resources by your team is efficient and takes into account the potential impact on the environment

d) you monitor the quality of resources continuously and ensure consistency in product and service delivery

e) you identify problems with resources promptly, and make recommendations for **corrective action** to the **relevant people** as soon as possible

f) you make recommendations for improving the use of resources to **relevant people** in an appropriate and timely manner

g) your records relating to the use of resources are complete, accurate and available to authorised people only.

Knowledge requirements

You need to know and understand

Communication
- how to communicate effectively with team members, colleagues and line managers

Involvement and motivation
- how to encourage others to take responsibility for the control of resources in their own area of work

Organisational context
- team objectives and organisational policies regarding the use of resources
- the potential environmental impact of the resources being used
- the problems which may occur with resources and how you can deal with these
- organisational procedures for making recommendations on the use of resources

Resource management
- the principles underpinning the effective and efficient management of resources
- how to monitor and control the use of resources to maximise efficiency, whilst maintaining the quality of products and services
- the importance of keeping accurate records on the use of resources.

Evidence requirements

You must prove that you *contribute to the control of resources* to the National Standard of competence.

To do this, you must provide evidence to convince your assessor that you consistently meet **all** the performance criteria.

Your evidence must be the result of real work activities undertaken by yourself. Evidence from simulated activities is **not** acceptable for this element.

You must show evidence that you give opportunities to take responsibility for the efficient use of resources to at least **one** of the following types of **relevant people**
- team members
- colleagues working at the same level as yourself.

You must also show evidence that you take at least **two** of the following types of **corrective action**
- altering activities
- modifying the use of resources
- renegotiating allocation of resources.

You must, however, convince your assessor that you have the necessary knowledge, understanding and skills to be able to perform competently in respect of **all** types of **relevant people** and **corrective action**, listed above.

Manage yourself

Unit summary

This unit is about developing your own skills and managing your time so that you can meet your objectives.

This unit contains two elements

C1.1 *Develop your own skills to improve your performance*

C1.2 *Manage your time to meet your objectives.*

Personal competencies

In performing effectively in this unit, you will show that you

Acting assertively
- take personal responsibility for making things happen
- say no to unreasonable requests

Communicating
- identify the information needs of listeners
- encourage listeners to ask questions or rephrase statements to clarify their understanding
- modify communication in response to feedback from listeners

Focusing on results
- maintain a focus on objectives
- tackle problems and take advantage of opportunities as they arise
- prioritise objectives and schedule work to make best use of time and resources

Managing self
- take responsibility for meeting your own learning and development needs
- seek feedback on performance to identify strengths and weaknesses
- learn from your own mistakes and those of others
- change behaviour where needed as a result of feedback

Thinking and taking decisions
- break processes down into tasks and activities
- identify implications, consequences or causal relationships in a situation
- produce a variety of solutions before taking a decision
- take decisions which are realistic for the situation.

Manage yourself

Element C1.1

Develop your own skills to improve your performance

Performance criteria

You must ensure that

a) you assess your skills and identify your development needs at appropriate intervals

b) your **assessment** takes account of the skills you need to work effectively with other team members

c) your plans for developing your skills are consistent with the needs you have identified

d) your plans for developing your skills contain specific, measurable and realistic objectives

e) you undertake development activities which are consistent with your plans for developing your skills

f) you obtain feedback from **relevant people** and use it to enhance your performance in the future

g) you update your plans for developing your skills at appropriate intervals.

Knowledge requirements

You need to know and understand

Communication
- the importance of getting feedback from others on your performance and how to encourage, enable and use such feedback in a constructive manner.

Management competence
- the principal skills required for effective managerial performance
- the types of interpersonal skills required for effective team work.

Organisational context
- the current and likely future requirements and standards within your job role and how they correspond to your level of competence as a manager
- the appropriate people from whom to get feedback on your performance.

Training and development
- the importance of continuing self-development to managerial competence
- how to assess your own current level of competence
- how to develop a personal action plan for learning and self-development with realistic objectives
- the types of development activities and their relative advantages and disadvantages
- how to assess your personal progress and update your plans accordingly.

Evidence requirements

You must prove that you *develop your own skills to improve your performance* to the National Standard of competence.

To do this, you must provide evidence to convince your assessor that you consistently meet **all** the performance criteria.

Your evidence must be the result of real work activities undertaken by yourself. Evidence from simulated activities is **not** acceptable for this element.

You must show evidence that your **assessments** take account of **all** of the following
- work objectives
- personal objectives
- organisational policies and requirements.

You must also show evidence that you obtain support and feedback from **two** of the following types of **relevant people**
- team members
- colleagues working at the same level as yourself
- higher-level managers or sponsors
- specialists.

You must, however, convince your assessor that you have the necessary knowledge, understanding and skills to be able to perform competently in respect of **all** types of **relevant people**, listed above.

Manage yourself

Manage your time to meet your objectives

Performance criteria

You must ensure that

a) your objectives are specific, measurable and achievable

b) you prioritise your objectives in line with organisational objectives and policies

c) you plan activities which are consistent with your objectives and your personal resources

d) your estimates of the time you need for activities are realistic and allow for unforeseen circumstances

e) you take decisions as soon as you have sufficient information

f) you minimise unhelpful interruptions to, and digressions from, planned work

g) you regularly review progress and reschedule activities to help achieve your planned objectives.

Knowledge requirements

You need to know and understand

Information handling
- how to assess how much information is required before an effective decision can be taken.

Monitoring and evaluation
- the importance of regular reviews of activity and rescheduling of work to achieving planned objectives.
- how to plan and carry out reviews.

Planning
- how to set objectives for yourself which are specific, measurable and achievable
- how to prioritise work in line with organisational objectives and policies
- how to estimate the amount of time required to carry out planned activities
- the kind of contingencies which may occur and how to assess and plan for these.

Time management
- the importance of effective time management to managerial competence
- how to identify and minimise unhelpful interruptions to planned work.

Evidence requirements

You must prove that you *manage your time to meet your objectives* to the National Standard of competence.

To do this, you must provide evidence to convince your assessor that you consistently meet **all** the performance criteria.

Your evidence must be the result of real work activities undertaken by yourself. Evidence from simulated activities is **not** acceptable for this element.

Create effective working relationships

Unit summary

This unit is about creating and maintaining effective working relationships with your manager, team members and other colleagues within your organisation. It also involves minimising the potential for conflict and dealing with conflicts when they arise.

This unit contains three elements

C4.1 *Gain the trust and support of colleagues and team members*
C4.2 *Gain the trust and support of your manager*
C4.3 *Minimise conflict in your team.*

Personal competencies

In performing effectively in this unit, you will show that you

Acting assertively
- take personal responsibility for making things happen
- say no to unreasonable requests

Building teams
- actively build relationships with others
- make time available to support others
- provide feedback designed to improve people's future performance
- show respect for the views and actions of others
- show sensitivity to the needs and feelings of others
- keep others informed about plans and progress

Communicating
- listen actively, ask questions, clarify points and rephrase others' statements to check mutual understanding
- identify the information needs of listeners
- adopt communication styles appropriate to listeners and situations, including selecting an appropriate time and place

Managing self
- accept personal comments or criticism without becoming defensive
- remain calm in difficult or uncertain situations
- handle others' emotions without becoming personally involved in them

Thinking and taking decisions
- reconcile and make use of a variety of perspectives when making sense of a situation
- produce your own ideas from experience and practice
- take decisions which are realistic for the situation
- focus on facts, problems and solutions when handling an emotional situation.

Create effective working
relationships

Element C4.1

Gain the trust and support of colleagues and team members

Performance criteria

You must ensure that

a) you consult with **colleagues** and **team members** about proposed activities at appropriate times and in a manner which encourages open, frank discussion

b) you keep **colleagues** and **team members** informed about organisational plans and activities

c) you honour the commitments you make to **colleagues** and **team members**

d) you treat **colleagues** and **team members** in a manner which shows your respect for individuals and the need for confidentiality

e) you give **colleagues** and **team members** sufficient support for them to achieve their work objectives

f) you discuss your evaluation of their work and behaviour directly with the **colleagues** and **team members** concerned.

Knowledge requirements

You need to know and understand

Communication
- how to consult with colleagues in a way which encourages open and frank discussions
- how to select communication methods appropriate to the issues and contexts
- the importance of effective communication methods to productive working relationships
- the importance of discussing evaluations of output and behaviour at work promptly and directly with those concerned
- how to provide feedback in a way which will lead to a constructive outcome.

Information handling
- the types of information concerning colleagues which you need to treat confidentially, and procedures to follow.

Organisational context
- the organisational plans and activities, emerging threats and opportunities, which are relevant to the work of colleagues and about which they need to be informed.

Providing support
- the support colleagues may require to achieve their objectives and how to provide this support.

Working relationships
- how people work in groups
- strategies and styles of working which encourage effective working relationships
- the importance of honouring commitments to colleagues
- the importance of showing respect for colleagues and how to do this.

Evidence requirements

You must prove that you *gain the trust and support of colleagues and team members* to the National Standard of competence.

To do this, you must provide evidence to convince your assessor that you consistently meet **all** the performance criteria.

Your evidence must be the result of real work activities undertaken by yourself. Evidence from simulated activities is **not** acceptable for this element.

You must show evidence of gaining the trust and support of **one** of the following types of **colleagues**
- those working at the same level as you
- those working at a higher level than you
- those working at a lower level than you.

You must also show evidence of gaining the trust and support of **one** of the following types of **team members**
- people for whom you have line management responsibility
- people for whom you have functional responsibility.

You must, however, convince your assessor that you have the necessary knowledge, understanding and skills to be able to perform competently in respect of **all** types of **colleagues** and **team members**, listed above.

Create effective working relationships

Gain the trust and support of your manager

Performance criteria

You must ensure that

a) you give your **manager** timely and accurate reports on activities, progress, results and achievements

b) you give your **manager** clear, accurate and timely information about emerging threats and opportunities

c) you consult your **manager** about organisational policies and ways of working at appropriate times

d) your **proposals** for action are clear and realistic

e) you present your **proposals** for action to your **manager** at appropriate times

f) where you have disagreements with your **manager**, you make constructive efforts to resolve these disagreements.

Knowledge requirements

You need to know and understand

Communication
- the importance of keeping your manager informed of activities, progress, results and achievements and how to do this
- how to develop and present proposals in ways which are realistic, clear and likely to influence your manager positively.

Organisational context
- the management structures, lines of accountability and control in your organisation
- the types of emerging threats and opportunities about which your manager needs to be informed
- the types of organisational policies and ways of working about which you need to consult with your manager and how to do this.

Working relationships
- strategies and styles of working which encourage effective working relationships
- methods of handling disagreements with your manager in a constructive manner.

Evidence requirements

You must prove that you *gain the trust and support of your manager* to the National Standard of competence.

To do this, you must provide evidence to convince your assessor that you consistently meet **all** the performance criteria.

Your evidence must be the result of real work activities undertaken by yourself. Evidence from simulated activities is acceptable **only** for performance criterion f) in this element.

You must show evidence that you gain the support of a **manager** who is **either**
- the person(s) to whom you report **or**
- the organisation or authority to which you report.

You must also show evidence that you present **proposals** in **one** of the following forms
- spoken
- written.

You must, however, convince your assessor that you have the necessary knowledge, understanding and skills to be able to perform competently in respect of **both** types of **managers** and **proposals**, listed above.

31

Create effective working
relationships

Element C4.3

Minimise conflict in your team

Performance criteria

You must ensure that

a) you inform **team members** of the standards of work and behaviour you expect, in a manner and at a level and pace appropriate to the individuals concerned

b) you provide appropriate opportunities for **team members** to discuss **problems** which directly or indirectly affect their work

c) you take action promptly to deal with conflict between **team members**

d) you inform relevant people about conflicts outside your area of responsibility

e) the way you resolve conflict minimises disruption to work and discord between **team members**

f) records of conflicts and their outcomes are accurate and comply with requirements for confidentiality and other organisational policies.

Knowledge requirements

You need to know and understand

Information handling
- the importance of maintaining accurate records of conflicts and their outcomes
- the information regarding conflicts which must be treated confidentially and the people who may and may not be informed.

Organisational context
- the people to inform when conflicts are outside your area of responsibility
- the organisational requirements regarding the handling of conflict and its resolution.

Working relationships
- situations, behaviour and interactions between people which encourage conflict
- how to minimise conflict between people at work
- the importance of keeping people regularly informed of expected standards of work and behaviour
- how to inform people of the standards and behaviour you expect of them
- the importance of giving people opportunities to discuss problems affecting their work and how to provide such opportunities
- how to identify potential conflict between individuals in your organisation
- types of conflict which may occur between people at work and action to take in response to these which will minimise disruption to work.

Evidence requirements

You must prove that you *minimise conflict in your team* to the National Standard of competence.

To do this, you must provide evidence to convince your assessor that you consistently meet **all** the performance criteria.

Your evidence must be the result of real work activities undertaken by yourself. Evidence from simulated activities is acceptable **only** for performance criteria c)–f) in this element.

You must show evidence of minimising conflict between **team members** who are **either**
- people for whom you have line management responsibility **or**
- people for whom you have functional responsibility.

You must show evidence of discussing **problems** which are **either**
- work related **or**
- personal.

You must, however, convince your assessor that you have the necessary knowledge, understanding and skills to be able to perform competently in respect of **both** types of **team members** and **problems**, listed above.

Manage information for action

Unit summary

This unit is about the efficient management of information within your area of responsibility. It covers gathering the information you need, providing information and advice to others, and holding meetings.

This unit contains three elements

D1.1 *Gather required information*
D1.2 *Inform and advise others*
D1.3 *Hold meetings*.

Personal competencies

In performing effectively in this unit, you will show that you

Acting assertively
- take a leading role in initiating action and making decisions
- act in an assured and unhesitating manner when faced with a challenge
- say no to unreasonable requests

Building teams
- actively build relationships with others
- show respect for the views and actions of others
- show sensitivity to the needs and feelings of others
- invite others to contribute to planning and organising work

Communicating
- listen actively, ask questions, clarify points and rephrase others' statements to check mutual understanding
- identify the information needs of listeners
- adopt communication styles appropriate to listeners and situations, including selecting an appropriate time and place
- use a variety of media and communication aids to reinforce points and maintain interest
- confirm listeners' understanding through questioning and interpretation of non-verbal signals
- encourage listeners to ask questions or rephrase statements to clarify their understanding
- modify communication in response to feedback from listeners

Influencing others
- present yourself positively to others
- use a variety of means to influence others

Searching for information
- establish information networks to search for and gather relevant information
- make best use of existing sources of information
- seek information from multiple sources
- challenge the validity and reliability of sources of information
- push for concrete information in an ambiguous situation

Thinking and taking decisions
- produce a variety of solutions before taking a decision
- reconcile and make use of a variety of perspectives when making sense of a situation
- produce your own ideas from experience and practice
- take decisions which are realistic for the situation.

Manage information for action

Element D1.1

Gather required information

Performance criteria

You must ensure that

a) the **information** you gather is accurate, sufficient and relevant to the purpose for which it is needed

b) you take prompt and effective action to overcome problems in gathering relevant **information**

c) you record and store the **information** you gather according to your organisation's **systems and procedures**

d) the **information** you gather is accessible in the required format to authorised people only

e) you identify possible improvements to **systems and procedures** and pass these on to the relevant people.

Knowledge requirements

You need to know and understand

Analytical techniques
- how to assess the effectiveness of current methods of gathering and storing information

Information handling
- the importance of gathering, validating and analysing information to team and organisational effectiveness and your role and responsibility in relation to this
- the types of qualitative and quantitative information which are essential to your role and responsibilities
- how to gather the information you need for your job
- the types of problems which may occur when gathering information and how to overcome these
- how to record and store the information you need

Organisational context
- the procedures to follow in order to make recommendations for improvements to systems and procedures.

Evidence requirements

You must prove that you *gather required information* to the National Standard of competence.

To do this, you must provide evidence to convince your assessor that you consistently meet **all** the performance criteria.

Your evidence must be the result of real work activities undertaken by yourself. Evidence from simulated activities is **not** acceptable for this element.

You must show evidence that you cover **both** of the following types of **information**
- quantitative
- qualitative.

You must also show evidence of using **one** of the following types of **systems and procedures**
- formal
- informal.

You must, however, convince your assessor that you have the necessary knowledge, understanding and skills to be able to perform competently in respect of **both** types of **systems and procedures** listed above.

Manage information for action

Element D1.2

Inform and advise others

Performance criteria

You must ensure that

a) you give **information and advice** at a time and place, and in a form and manner, appropriate to the needs of **recipients**

b) the **information** you give is accurate, current, relevant and sufficient

c) the **advice** you give is consistent with your organisation's policy, procedures and resource constraints

d) you use reasoned arguments and appropriate evidence to support your **advice**

e) you check and confirm **recipients'** understanding of the **information and advice** you have given them

f) you maintain confidentiality according to your organisation's requirements

g) you seek feedback from **recipients** about the **information and advice** you provide, and use this feedback to improve the ways in which you give **information and advice**.

Knowledge requirements

You need to know and understand

Communication
- how to give information and advice effectively both orally and in writing
- how to develop and present a reasoned case when providing advice to others
- the importance of confirming the recipient's understanding of the information and advice you have provided and how to do this
- the importance of seeking feedback on the quality and relevance of the advice and information you provided, and how to encourage and enable such feedback

Information handling
- the importance of providing information and advice to others and your role and responsibility in relation to this
- the types of information and advice which other people may require
- the importance of checking the validity of information and advice provided to others and how to do this
- the principles of confidentiality when handling information and advice; the types of information and advice which may be provided to different people

Organisational context
- organisational policies, procedures and resource constraints which may affect advice and information you give to others.

Evidence requirements

You must prove that you *inform and advise others* to the National Standard of competence.

To do this, you must provide evidence to convince your assessor that you consistently meet **all** the performance criteria.

Your evidence must be the result of real work activities undertaken by yourself. Evidence from simulated activities is **not** acceptable for this element.

You must show evidence of providing **both** of the following forms of **information and advice**
- spoken
- written.

You must also show evidence of providing information and advice to **two** of the following types of **recipients**
- team members
- colleagues working at the same level
- higher-level managers or sponsors
- people not part of your organisation.

You must, however, convince your assessor that you have the necessary knowledge, understanding and skills to be able to perform competently in respect of **all** types of **recipients** listed above.

Manage information for action

Hold meetings

Performance criteria

You must ensure that

a) you give sufficient notice of the **meeting** to allow the necessary people to attend

b) you make clear the **purpose** and objectives of the **meeting** at the start

c) your style of leadership helps people to make useful contributions

d) you discourage unhelpful arguments and digressions

e) the **meeting** achieves its objectives within the allocated time

f) you give clear, accurate and concise information about outcomes of the **meeting** promptly to those who need it.

Knowledge requirements

You need to know and understand

Communication
- how to identify unhelpful arguments and digressions, and strategies which may be used to discourage these

Leadership styles
- the styles of leadership which can be used to run meetings and how to choose a style according the nature of the meeting

Meetings
- the value and limitations of meetings as a method of exchanging information and making decisions
- how to determine when a meeting is the most effective way of dealing with issues; the possible alternatives which you may use
- the importance of determining the purpose and objectives of meetings and how to do so
- how to manage discussions so that the objectives of the meeting are met within the allocated time

Organisational context
- how to determine who are the necessary people to attend the meeting
- procedures to follow when calling meetings and preparing for them.

Evidence requirements

You must prove that you *hold meetings* to the National Standard of competence.

To do this, you must provide evidence to convince your assessor that you consistently meet **all** the performance criteria.

Your evidence must be the result of real work activities undertaken by yourself. Evidence from simulated activities is **not** acceptable for this element.

You must show evidence of holding **one** of the following types of **meetings**
- involving people within your organisation
- involving people outside your organisation.

You must also show evidence of holding meetings with **one** of the following types of **purpose**
- information giving
- consultation
- decision making.

You must, however, convince your assessor that you have the necessary knowledge, understanding and skills to be able to perform competently in respect of **all** types of **meetings** and **purposes** listed above.

Management

Level 3

NVQ/SVQ

Optional units
Candidates take TWO optional units

Contribute to the selection of personnel for activities

Unit summary

This unit is about making a significant contribution to selecting the people needed to carry out your work activities. It applies to both the external and internal recruitment of people for permanent, temporary or project work. It applies equally to paid or voluntary work, whether full-time or part-time.

This unit contains two elements

C7.1 *Contribute to identifying personnel requirements*
C7.2 *Contribute to selecting required personnel.*

Personal competencies

In performing effectively in this unit, you will show that you

Acting assertively
- state your own position and views clearly in conflict situations
- maintain your own beliefs, commitment and effort in spite of set-backs and opposition

Behaving ethically
- comply with legislation, industry regulation, professional and organisational codes
- show integrity and fairness in decision-making

Communicating
- listen actively, ask questions, clarify points and rephrase others' statements and check mutual understanding
- adopt communication styles appropriate to listeners and situations, including selecting an appropriate time and place
- confirm listeners' understanding through questioning and interpretation of non-verbal signals
- encourage listeners to ask questions or rephrase statements to clarify their understanding
- modify communication in response to feedback from listeners

Influencing others
- present yourself positively to others
- create and prepare strategies for influencing others
- understand the culture of your organisation and act to work within it or influence it

Searching for information
- actively encourage the free exchange of information
- make best use of existing sources of information
- seek information from multiple sources
- challenge the validity and reliability of sources of information
- push for concrete information in an ambiguous situation

Thinking and taking decisions
- break processes down into tasks and activities
- identify patterns or meaning from events and data which are not obviously related
- take decisions which are realistic for the situation.

Contribute to the selection of
personnel for activities

Element C7.1

Contribute to identifying personnel requirements

Performance criteria

You must ensure that

a) you base your contributions to identifying **personnel requirements** on current, valid and reliable information

b) your contributions take account of **work objectives and constraints**

c) the **personnel requirements** you suggest meet organisational needs and legal requirements

d) you present your contributions to relevant people in the agreed format at the agreed time.

Knowledge requirements

You need to know and understand

Communication
- how to make a case for additional personnel needs in a way which is likely to influence decision-makers positively.

Information handling
- how to collect and check the validity of the information necessary to contribute to personnel requirements.

Legal requirements
- the legal requirements for the identification of personnel specifications.

Organisational context
- the organisational requirements for identifying personnel needs.

Recruitment and selection
- how to identify and interpret the work objectives and constraints which are relevant to identifying your personnel needs
- how to help specify the job roles, competences and attributes required to meet these needs.

Evidence requirements

You must prove that you *contribute to identifying personnel requirements* to the National Standard of competence.

To do this, you must provide evidence to convince your assessor that you consistently meet **all** the performance criteria.

Your evidence must be the result of real work activities undertaken by yourself. Evidence from simulated activities is **not** acceptable for this element.

You must show evidence that you contribute to identifying requirements for at least **four** of the following types of **personnel**
- internal
- external
- permanent
- temporary
- full-time
- part-time
- paid
- voluntary.

You must also show evidence that you contribute to identifying **all** of the following types of **requirements**
- skills
- knowledge
- personal attributes.

You must also show evidence that you take account of at least **two** of the following types of **work objectives and constraints**
- work plans, targets and commitments
- staff availability
- organisational values and policies
- financial considerations
- industry-specific requirements.

You must, however, convince your assessor that you have the necessary knowledge, understanding and skills to be able to perform competently in respect of **all** types of **personnel** and **work objectives and constraints**, listed above.

Contribute to the selection of
personnel for activities

Element C7.2

Contribute to selecting required personnel

Performance criteria

You must ensure that

a) the **methods** you use to assess and select **personnel** meet organisational requirements

b) the information which you provide is complete, accurate and supports the fair assessment of **personnel**

c) your suggestions for the selection of **personnel** are based on objective assessments of the information against agreed selection criteria

d) your suggestions for selection are clear and accurate

e) you make your suggestions available only to **authorised people**

f) you handle your communications with **personnel** in a manner and at a level and pace appropriate to their needs

g) your records of your contribution to the selection process are complete, accurate, clear and meet organisational requirements.

Knowledge requirements

You need to know and understand

Communication

- how to present suggestions for selection effectively
- how to communicate effectively with the range of personnel involved.

Information handling

- the importance of confidentiality during selection processes – what kinds of information may be made known to which staff
- the importance of keeping accurate, complete and clear records of one's contributions to the selection process.

Legal requirements

- legal requirements for the selection of personnel.

Organisational context

- organisational requirements for the selection of personnel.

Recruitment and selection

- the range of methods which may be used for the assessment and selection of staff and the relative advantages and disadvantages of these for your team
- the contributions you can make to the assessment and selection of staff
- how to make fair and objective assessments against criteria during the selection process.

Evidence requirements

You must prove that you *contribute to selecting required personnel* to the National Standard of competence.

To do this, you must provide evidence to convince your assessor that you consistently meet **all** the performance criteria.

Your evidence must be the result of real work activities undertaken by yourself. Evidence from simulated activities is **not** acceptable for this element.

You must also show evidence that you contribute to the selection of at least **four** of the following types of **personnel**

- internal
- permanent
- full-time
- paid
- external
- temporary
- part-time
- voluntary.

You must also show evidence that you contribute to at least **two** of the following types of assessment and selection **methods**

- analysis of written applications
- interviews
- tests of work skills.

You must also show evidence that you make your selection suggestions to at least **two** of the following types of **authorised people**

- colleagues working at the same level
- higher-level managers or sponsors
- personnel specialists
- members of the selection board.

You must, however, convince your assessor that you have the necessary knowledge, understanding and skills to be able to perform competently in respect of **all** types of assessment and selection **methods**, **personnel** and **authorised people**, listed above.

Contribute to the development of teams and individuals

Unit summary

This unit is about making a significant contribution to developing the knowledge and skills of individuals and teams to ensure that they produce the best possible results at work. It covers helping to identify people's development needs, planning to meet those needs, carrying out development activities and assessing members of your team to see how they have progressed.

This unit contains four elements

C9.1 *Contribute to the identification of development needs*
C9.2 *Contribute to planning the development of teams and individuals*
C9.3 *Contribute to development activities*
C9.4 *Contribute to the assessment of people against development objectives.*

Personal competencies

In performing effectively in this unit, you will show that you

Acting assertively
- state your own position and views clearly in conflict situations
- maintain your beliefs, commitment and effort in spite of set-backs or opposition

Building teams
- make time available to support others
- encourage and stimulate others to make the best use of their abilities
- evaluate and enhance people's capability to do their jobs
- provide feedback designed to improve people's future performance
- use power and authority in a fair and equitable manner
- keep others informed about plans and progress
- invite others to contribute to planning and organising work
- set objectives which are both achievable and challenging

Communicating
- listen actively, ask questions, clarify points and rephrase others' statements to check mutual understanding
- identify the information needs of listeners
- adopt communication styles appropriate to listeners and situations, including selecting an appropriate time and place
- use a variety of media and communication aids to reinforce points and maintain interest
- present difficult ideas and problems in ways that promote understanding
- confirm listeners' understanding through questioning and interpretation of non-verbal signals
- encourage listeners to ask questions or rephrase statements to clarify their understanding
- modify communication in response to feedback from listeners

Thinking and taking decisions
- break processes down into tasks and activities
- use your own experience and evidence from others to identify problems and understand situations
- take decisions which are realistic for the situation.

Contribute to the development
of teams and individuals

Element C9.1

Contribute to the identification of development needs

Performance criteria

You must ensure that

a) you give opportunities to team members
   to help identify their own **development
   needs**

b) you identify their **development needs**
   accurately and use sufficient, reliable
   and valid information

c) the **development needs** you identify
   are consistent with team objectives and
   organisational values

d) you present information on
   development needs to **authorised
   people** only, in the required format and
   to agreed deadlines.

Knowledge requirements

You need to know and understand

Communication
- how to present development needs to people in a way which is likely to influence their decision-making positively.

Continuous improvement
- the importance of team development to the continuing effectiveness of your organisation and your role and responsibilities in contributing to this.

Information handling
- how to collect and validate the information needed to identify development needs.

Involvement and motivation
- the importance of providing team members with opportunities to help identify their own development needs
- how to encourage and enable team members to identify their development needs.

Organisational context
- team objectives and organisational values which have a bearing on development needs
- how to decide whether development needs are consistent with organisational objectives and values.

Training and development
- how to identify development needs in the team
- what information is needed to identify development needs.

Evidence requirements

You must prove that you *contribute to the identification of development needs* to the National Standard of competence.

To do this, you must provide evidence to convince your assessor that you consistently meet **all** the performance criteria.

Your evidence must be the result of real work activities undertaken by yourself. Evidence from simulated activities is **not** acceptable for this element.

You must show evidence that you identify **both** of the following types of **development needs**
- to meet team objectives
- to meet individual aspirations.

You must also show evidence that you present the necessary information to at least **two** of the following types of **authorised people**
- team members
- colleagues working at the same level as yourself
- higher-level managers or sponsors
- specialists.

You must, however, convince your assessor that you have the necessary knowledge, understanding and skills to be able to perform competently in respect of **all** aspects of the **authorised people**, listed above.

Contribute to the development
of teams and individuals

Element C9.2

Contribute to planning the development of teams and individuals

Performance criteria

You must ensure that

a) your contributions to the planning process reflect the identified **development needs** of all those you are responsible for

b) your contributions are clear, relevant, realistic and take account of team and organisational constraints

c) you agree your ideas with individual team members, taking account of their work activities, learning abilities and personal circumstances

d) you present your contributions to **authorised people** only, in the required format and to agreed deadlines.

Knowledge requirements

You need to know and understand

Involvement and motivation

- the importance of agreeing development plans with those involved and how to reach such agreements.

Organisational context

- the team and organisational constraints which influence the planning of development activities.

Training and development

- how to contribute to planning the development of teams and individuals
- the training needs you have identified and how your contributions to the planning process will help meet these needs
- how to take account of team and organisational constraints in the planning process
- the importance of taking account of team members' work activities, their learning abilities and personal circumstances and how to build these factors into development activities
- the correct procedures for presenting your contributions to planning development activities.

Evidence requirements

You must prove that you *contribute to planning the development of teams and individuals* to the National Standard of competence.

To do this, you must provide evidence to convince your assessor that you consistently meet **all** the performance criteria.

Your evidence must be the result of real work activities undertaken by yourself. Evidence from simulated activities is **not** acceptable for this element.

You must show evidence that your contributions meet **both** of the following types of **development needs**

- to meet organisational objectives
- to meet individual aspirations.

You must also show evidence that you present your contributions to at least **two** of the following types of **authorised people**

- team members
- colleagues working at the same level as yourself
- higher-level managers or sponsors
- specialists.

You must, however, convince your assessor that you have the necessary knowledge, understanding and skills to be able to perform competently in respect of **all** types of **authorised people**, listed above.

Contribute to the development
of teams and individuals

Element C9.3

Contribute to development activities

Performance criteria

You must ensure that

a) your **contributions** to development activities support your team objectives and plans

b) your **contributions** meet the agreed objectives of the development activity

c) your **contributions** take into account the work activities, learning abilities and personal circumstances of your individual team members

d) you encourage and use feedback from those taking part in the activities to improve your future **contributions** to development activities.

Knowledge requirements

You need to know and understand

Continuous improvement

- the importance of monitoring and reviewing development activities and taking note of feedback from those who are taking part
- how to encourage and gather useful feedback from team members on the development activities they are involved in.

Training and development

- the types of contributions which you could make to development activities for your team members
- how to choose contributions which are appropriate to your team members, the type of development activity which is planned and your own abilities and objectives
- how to ensure your own contribution is meeting agreed objectives and plans for the activities
- why development activities should take account of team members' work activities, their learning abilities and personal circumstances.

Evidence requirements

You must prove that you *contribute to development activities* to the National Standard of competence.

To do this, you must provide evidence to convince your assessor that you consistently meet **all** the performance criteria.

Your evidence must be the result of real work activities undertaken by yourself. Evidence from simulated activities is **not** acceptable for this element.

You must show evidence that you make at least **three** of the following types of **contributions**

- providing information to team members
- instructing team members in aspects of their work
- skills training
- providing learning opportunities at work
- providing feedback on their work.

You must, however, convince your assessor that you have the necessary knowledge, understanding and skills to be able to perform competently in respect of **all** types of **contributions**, listed above.

Contribute to the development
of teams and individuals

Element C9.4

Contribute to the assessment of people against development objectives

Performance criteria

You must ensure that

a) you agree the **purpose** of the **assessment** and your role in it with relevant people

b) you give opportunities to team members to contribute to their own **assessments**

c) you give equal access to all team members to be assessed against development objectives

d) you carry out your role in the **assessments** objectively against clear, agreed criteria

e) you base your **assessments** on sufficient, valid and reliable information

f) you provide information about **assessments** to authorised people only, in the required format and to agreed deadlines.

Knowledge requirements

You need to know and understand

Information handling
- the information needed to assess team members' progress
- how to collect and check the validity of information
- the importance of confidentiality when carrying out and reporting assessments – what types of information should be provided to which people.

Involvement and motivation
- the importance of team members contributing to the assessment of their own progress
- how to encourage and enable them to do so.

Organisational context
- the organisational procedures for reporting the results of assessment.

Training and development
- the importance of assessing team members' development
- the range of purposes which the assessment may have
- the importance of agreeing the purpose of the assessment with team members, line managers, colleagues and specialists
- the importance of fair and objective assessment
- how to assess team members' progress against development objectives
- methods which may be used to assess the progress of team members objectively and fairly.

Evidence requirements

You must prove that you *contribute to the assessment of people against development objectives* to the National Standard of competence.

To do this, you must provide evidence to convince your assessor that you consistently meet **all** the performance criteria.

Your evidence must be the result of real work activities undertaken by yourself. Evidence from simulated activities is **not** acceptable for this element.

You must show evidence that your assessments have at least **two** of the following types of **purpose**
- identification of further training and development needs
- evaluation of the effectiveness of the training and development process
- appraisal of performance
- recognition of knowledge, skills and competence at work.

You must show evidence that you carry out at least **two** of the following types of **assessments**
- testing of knowledge and skills
- observation of performance at work
- appraisal discussions.

You must also show evidence that you agree the purpose of and provide information about **assessment** to at least **two** of the following
- teams and individuals being assessed
- higher-level managers or sponsors
- colleagues working at the same level as yourself
- specialists.

You must, however, convince your assessor that you have the necessary knowledge, understanding and skills to be able to perform competently in respect of **all** types of **purposes** and **assessments**, listed above.

Lead the work of teams and individuals to achieve their objectives

Unit summary

This unit is about making best use of your team and its members so that they can achieve their objectives. It covers planning and assessing work, and providing feedback to team members.

This unit contains three elements

C12.1 *Plan the work of teams and individuals*
C12.2 *Assess the work of teams and individuals*
C12.3 *Provide feedback to teams and individuals on their work.*

Personal competencies

In performing effectively in this unit, you will show that you

Acting assertively
- take a leading role in initiating action and making decisions
- take personal responsibility for making things happen
- take control of situations and events

Building teams
- actively build relationships with others
- make time available to support others
- encourage and stimulate others to make the best use of their abilities
- evaluate and enhance people's capability to do their jobs
- provide feedback designed to improve people's future performance
- show respect for the views and actions of others
- show sensitivity to the needs and feelings of others
- use power and authority in a fair and equitable manner
- keep others informed about plans and progress
- clearly identify what is required of others
- invite others to contribute to planning and organising work
- set objectives which are both achievable and challenging
- check individuals' commitment to a specific course of action
- use a variety of techniques to promote morale and productivity
- identify and resolve causes of conflict or resistance

Communicating
- listen actively, ask questions, clarify points and rephrase others' statements to check mutual understanding
- adopt communication styles appropriate to listeners and situations, including selecting an appropriate time and place
- confirm listeners' understanding through questioning and interpretation of non-verbal signals
- modify communication in response to feedback from listeners

Thinking and taking decisions
- break processes down into tasks and activities
- take decisions which are realistic for the situation.

Lead the work of teams and
individuals to achieve their
objectives

Element C12.1

Plan the work of teams and individuals

Performance criteria

You must ensure that

a) you give opportunities to your **team members** to contribute to the planning and organisation of their work

b) your **plans** are consistent with your team's objectives

c) your **plans** cover all those personnel whose work you are responsible for

d) your **plans** and schedules are realistic and achievable within **organisational constraints**

e) your **plans** and the way you allocate work take full account of **team members'** abilities and development needs

f) you explain to your **team members** your **plans** and their work activities in sufficient detail and at a level and pace appropriate to them

g) you confirm your **team members'** understanding of your **plans** and their work activities at appropriate times

h) you update your **plans** at regular intervals and take account of individual, team and organisational changes.

Knowledge requirements

You need to know and understand

Communication
- the importance of effective communication when explaining work plans and allocations
- how to present work plans in a way that gains the support and commitment of those involved.

Continuous improvement
- the importance of regularly reviewing work.

Involvement and motivation
- the importance of providing your team members with the opportunity to contribute to the planning and organisation of their work.

Organisational context
- the types of organisational constraints which influence your planning.

Planning
- the importance of planning work activities to organisational effectiveness and your role and responsibilities in relation to this
- how to develop realistic and achievable work plans for teams and individuals both in the short and medium term
- the team's objectives and how your plans succeed in meeting these.

Working relationships
- the difference between someone who is within your line management control and someone for whom you have functional responsibility, and the implications this difference may have for planning work.

Evidence requirements

You must prove that you *plan the work of teams and individuals* to the National Standard of competence.

To do this, you must provide evidence to convince your assessor that you consistently meet **all** the performance criteria.

Your evidence must be the result of real work activities undertaken by yourself. Evidence from simulated activities is **not** acceptable for this element.

You must show evidence that you involve and plan work for at least **one** of the following types of **team members**
- people for whom you have line responsibility
- people for whom you have functional responsibility.

You must also show evidence that you develop **both** of the following types of **plans**
- short-term
- medium-term.

You must show evidence that you take account of **all** of the following types of **organisational constraints**
- organisational objectives
- organisational policies
- resources.

You must, however, convince your assessor that you have the necessary knowledge, understanding and skills to be able to perform competently in respect of **all** types of **team members**, listed above.

UNIT C12

Lead the work of teams and
individuals to achieve their
objectives

Element C12.2

Assess the work of teams and individuals

Performance criteria

You must ensure that

a) you explain the **purpose** of
   assessment clearly to all involved

b) you give opportunities to team members
   to **assess** their own work

c) your **assessment** of work takes place at
   times most likely to maintain and
   improve effective performance

d) your **assessments** are based on
   sufficient, valid and reliable
   information

e) you make your **assessments** objectively
   against clear and agreed criteria.

Knowledge requirements

You need to know and understand

Communication

- the importance of being clear yourself about the purpose of assessment and of communicating this effectively to those involved.

Continuous improvement

- the importance of assessing the ongoing work of teams and individuals and your role and responsibilities in relation to this.

Information handling

- how to gather and evaluate the information you need to assess the work of teams and individuals.

Involvement and motivation

- the importance of providing opportunities to your team members to assess their own work and how you can encourage and enable this involvement.

Monitoring and evaluation

- the range of purposes of work assessment, why work assessment may play a role in an organisation and how they apply to your own situation
- how to assess the work of teams and individuals, and processes in the workplace which can support such assessment
- the principles of fair and objective assessment of work and how to ensure this is achieved.

Evidence requirements

You must prove that you *assess the work of teams and individuals* to the National Standard of competence.

To do this, you must provide evidence to convince your assessor that you consistently meet **all** the performance criteria.

Your evidence must be the result of real work activities undertaken by yourself. Evidence from simulated activities is **not** acceptable for this element.

You must show evidence that your assessments have at least **two** of the following types of **purpose**

- assuring that objectives have been achieved
- assuring that quality and customer requirements have been met
- appraising team or individual performance
- recognising competent performance and achievement.

You must show evidence that you use at least **one** of the following types of **assessment**

- specific to one activity or objective
- general to overall performance of the team or individual.

You must also show evidence that you base your **assessments** on **both** of the following types of **information**

- qualitative
- quantitative.

You must, however, convince your assessor that you have the necessary knowledge, understanding and skills to be able to perform competently in respect of **all** types of **purpose** and **assessment**, listed above.

Lead the work of teams and individuals to achieve their objectives

Element C12.3

Provide feedback to teams and individuals on their work

Performance criteria

You must ensure that

a) you provide **feedback** to your team members in a **situation** and in a **form** and manner most likely to maintain and improve performance

b) the **feedback** you give is clear and is based on an objective assessment of your team members' work

c) your **feedback** recognises team members' achievements and provides constructive suggestions and encouragement for improving their work

d) the way you give **feedback** shows respect for the individuals involved

e) you treat all **feedback** to individuals and teams confidentially

f) you give opportunities to team members to respond to **feedback** and recommend how they could improve their work.

Knowledge requirements

You need to know and understand

Communication

- the importance of good communication skills when providing feedback
- how to provide both positive and negative feedback to team members on their performance
- how to choose an appropriate time and a place to give feedback to teams and individuals
- how to provide feedback in a way which encourages your team members to feel that you respect them.

Continuous improvement

- the importance of providing clear and accurate feedback to your team members on their performance and your role and responsibilities in relation to this.

Information handling

- the principles of confidentiality when providing feedback – which people should receive which pieces of information.

Involvement and motivation

- how to motivate team members and gain their commitment by providing feedback
- the importance of being encouraging when providing feedback to team members and showing respect for those involved
- why it is important to provide constructive suggestions on how performance can be improved
- the importance of giving those involved the opportunity to provide suggestions on how to improve their work.

Evidence requirements

You must prove that you *provide feedback to teams and individuals on their work* to the National Standard of competence.

To do this, you must provide evidence to convince your assessor that you consistently meet **all** the performance criteria.

Your evidence must be the result of real work activities undertaken by yourself. Evidence from simulated activities is **not** acceptable for this element.

You must show evidence that you provide **both** of the following types of **feedback**
- positive
- negative.

You must also show evidence that you use **both** of the following **forms** of feedback
- spoken
- written.

You must show evidence that you give feedback in at least **two** of the following types of **situation**
- during normal day-to-day activities
- when required to maintain motivation, morale and effectiveness
- during formal appraisals
- at team meetings and briefings
- during confidential discussions of work.

You must, however, convince your assessor that you have the necessary knowledge, understanding and skills to be able to perform competently in respect of **all** types of **situation**, listed above.

Respond to poor performance in your team

Unit summary

This unit is about helping to deal with team members whose performance is unsatisfactory. It covers identifying their problems and providing help to deal with them. It also covers contributing to disciplinary and grievance procedures when work is consistently below standard or if a team member has a serious complaint against your organisation or someone in it.

This unit contains two elements

C15.1 *Help team members who have problems affecting their performance*
C15.2 *Contribute to implementing disciplinary and grievance procedures.*

Personal competencies

In performing effectively in this unit, you will show that you

Acting assertively
- act in an assured and unhesitating manner when faced with a challenge
- state your own position and views clearly in conflict situations
- maintain your beliefs, commitment and effort in spite of set-backs or opposition

Behaving ethically
- comply with legislation, industry regulation, professional and organisational codes
- show integrity and fairness in decision-making

Building teams
- make time available to support others
- encourage and stimulate others to make the best use of their abilities
- show respect for the views and actions of others
- show sensitivity to the needs and feelings of others
- use power and authority in a fair and equitable manner
- clearly identify what is required of others
- check individuals' commitment to a specific course of action
- use a variety of techniques to promote morale and productivity
- identify and resolve causes of conflict or resistance

Communicating
- listen actively, ask questions, clarify points and rephrase others' statements to check mutual understanding
- confirm listeners' understanding through questioning and interpretation of non-verbal signals
- encourage listeners to ask questions or rephrase statements to clarify their understanding
- modify communication in response to feedback from listeners

Focusing on results
- maintain a focus on objectives
- establish and communicate high expectations of performance, including setting an example to others
- monitor quality of work and progress against plans
- continually strive to identify and minimise barriers to excellence.

Respond to poor performance
in your team

Element C15.1

Help team members who have problems affecting their performance

Performance criteria

You must ensure that

a) you promptly identify poor performance and bring it directly to the attention of the **team member** concerned

b) you give the **team member** the opportunity to discuss actual or potential **problems** affecting their performance

c) you discuss these issues with the **team member** at a time and place appropriate to the type, seriousness and complexity of the **problem**

d) you gather and check as much information as possible to identify the nature of the **problem**

e) you agree with the **team member** a course of action which is appropriate, timely and effective

f) where necessary, you refer the **team member** to support services appropriate to their individual circumstances

g) the way you respond to **team members' problems** maintains respect for the individual and the need for confidentiality

h) you promptly inform relevant people of **problems** beyond your level of responsibility or competence.

Knowledge requirements

You need to know and understand

Communication
- the importance of providing opportunities for team members to discuss problems
- how to encourage and enable team members to talk frankly about their problems.

Information handling
- the importance of confidentiality.

Monitoring and evaluation
- the importance of promptly identifying poor performance and bringing it directly to team members' attention.

Providing support
- your role and responsibilities in dealing with team members' problems
- the types of problems which your team members may encounter at work
- how to identify problems which the individual is experiencing and devise appropriate responses
- the importance of agreeing a course of action with the team member involved
- how to decide when the problem goes beyond your own level of competence and responsibility
- the range of support services which exists inside and outside your organisation.

Working relationships
- the importance of maintaining respect for the individual
- the limits beyond which you should not go in becoming involved in the individual's problem.

Evidence requirements

You must prove that you *help team members who have problems affecting their performance* to the National Standard of competence.

To do this, you must provide evidence to convince your assessor that you consistently meet **all** the performance criteria.

Your evidence must be the result of real work activities undertaken by yourself. Evidence from simulated activities is **only** acceptable for performance criterion f) in this element.

You must show evidence that you help at least **one** of the following types of **team members**
- people for whom you have line management responsibility
- people for whom you have functional responsibility.

You must also show evidence that you help team members with at least **one** of the following types of **problems**
- arising from work-related factors
- arising from external personal factors.

You must, however, convince your assessor that you have the necessary knowledge, understanding and skills to be able to perform competently in respect of **all** types of **team members** and **problems**, listed above.

Respond to poor performance in your team

Contribute to implementing disciplinary and grievance procedures

Performance criteria

You must ensure that

a) your team members have clear, accurate and timely **information** regarding disciplinary and grievance procedures

b) your **contributions** to disciplinary and grievance procedures are provided in a fair, impartial and timely way

c) your **contributions** to implementing disciplinary and grievance procedures are consistent with your level of authority

d) your **contributions** to implementing disciplinary and grievance procedures maintain respect for the individual and the need for confidentiality.

Knowledge requirements

You need to know and understand

Disciplinary and grievance procedures

- the importance of effectively applying disciplinary and grievance procedures and your responsibilities in relation to this
- situations in which disciplinary and grievance procedures should be implemented
- the importance of informing team members about disciplinary and grievance procedures, appropriate times to do so and methods to use
- the importance of fairness, impartiality and responding in a timely way when dealing with disciplinary and grievance procedures.

Information handling

- the importance of confidentiality when dealing with disciplinary and grievance procedures – who may receive what information.

Legal requirements

- legal requirements relevant to disciplinary and grievance procedures.

Organisational context

- organisational requirements relevant to disciplinary and grievance procedures.

Working relationships

- the importance of maintaining respect for the individual when dealing with disciplinary and grievance procedures.

Evidence requirements

You must prove that you *contribute to implementing disciplinary and grievance procedures* to the National Standard of competence.

To do this, you must provide evidence to convince your assessor that you consistently meet **all** the performance criteria.

Your evidence should be the result of real work activities undertaken by yourself. However, evidence from simulated activities **is** acceptable for this element.

You must show evidence that you provide **both** of the following types of **information**
- organisational
- legal.

You must also show evidence that you make at least **one** of the following types of **contributions**
- requested by others
- on your own initiative.

You must, however, convince your assessor that you have the necessary knowledge, understanding and skills to be able to perform competently in respect of **both** types of **contributions**, listed above.

Identify improvements to energy efficiency

Unit summary

This unit is about helping the organisation improve its energy efficiency. It covers both identifying opportunities for improvement and making appropriate recommendations.

This unit contains two elements

E5.1 *Identify opportunities to improve energy efficiency*
E5.2 *Recommend improvements to energy efficiency.*

Personal competencies

In performing effectively in this unit, you will show that you

Communicating
- listen actively, ask questions, clarify points and rephrase others' statements to check mutual understanding
- identify the information needs of listeners
- adopt communication styles appropriate to listeners and situations, including selecting an appropriate time and place

Influencing others
- develop and use contacts to trade information, and obtain support and resources
- present yourself positively to others
- create and prepare strategies for influencing others
- use a variety of means to influence others
- understand the culture of your organisation and act to work within it or influence it

Searching for information
- establish information networks to search for and gather relevant information
- make best use of existing sources of information
- seek information from multiple sources
- challenge the validity and reliability of sources of information

Thinking and taking decisions
- break processes down into tasks and activities
- identify a range of elements in and perspectives on a situation
- identify implications, consequences or causal relationships in a situation
- use your own experience and evidence from others to identify problems and understand situations
- identify patterns or meanings from events and data which are not obviously related
- reconcile and make use of a variety of perspectives when making sense of a situation
- produce your own ideas from experience and practice
- take decisions which are realistic for the situation.

Identify improvements to
energy efficiency

Element E5.1

Identify opportunities to improve energy efficiency

Performance criteria

You must ensure that

a) you consistently identify developments and advances in energy efficiency best practice which are relevant to the organisation

b) you regularly identify new markets, products, services and technological innovations which offer improvements in energy efficiency

c) you regularly review **resources**, systems and operational activities to identify **opportunities** for improved energy efficiency

d) you select and use **resources** which optimise the use of energy throughout the organisation

e) you identify **opportunities** for recycling energy used for operational activities

f) you identify **external programmes** which support the organisation's energy efficiency initiatives

g) you encourage individuals and teams to identify **opportunities** which improve energy efficiency and contribute to a sustainable environment.

Knowledge requirements

You need to know and understand

Communication
- the principles and processes of effective communication and how to apply them

Energy efficiency
- how to identify opportunities for improved energy efficiency
- the principal developments and advances in energy efficiency best practice
- how to select and use resources which optimise energy use
- the range of new markets, products, services and technological innovations relevant to energy efficiency
- the principal energy recycling opportunities
- the range of external programmes which may support energy efficiency initiatives
- the main sources of information on developments in energy efficiency technology and best practice and how to make use of them

Environmental management
- the principle of sustainable development and how to work towards it

Involvement and motivation
- how to encourage individuals and teams to identify energy efficiency improvements

Organisational context
- organisational activities, systems and resources and their impact on energy efficiency.

Evidence requirements

You must prove that you *identify opportunities to improve energy efficiency* to the National Standard of competence.

To do this, you must provide evidence to convince your assessor that you consistently meet **all** the performance criteria.

Your evidence must be the result of real work activities undertaken by yourself. Evidence from simulated activities is **not** acceptable for this element.

You must show evidence that you review at least **two** of the following types of **resources**
- money
- people
- premises
- equipment
- materials
- energy.

You must show evidence that you identify at least **two** of the following types of **opportunities**
- products
- services
- technological innovation
- design and modification of systems
- equipment and buildings
- recycling
- insulation.

You must also show evidence that you identify at least **two** of the following types of **external programmes**
- grant aid
- environmental measures
- local
- national and EU conservation initiatives
- Best Practice Programme.

You must, however, convince your assessor that you have the necessary knowledge, understanding and skills to be able to perform competently in respect of **all** types of **resources, opportunities** and **external programmes** listed above.

Identify improvements to
energy efficiency

Element E5.2

Recommend improvements to energy efficiency

Performance criteria

You must ensure that

a) you accurately evaluate the **advantages and disadvantages** to the organisation of possible energy efficiency improvements

b) you assess advances in technology for their applicability to the organisation's systems and activities

c) you accurately evaluate alternative energy sources and suppliers for cost savings and energy efficiency

d) you make recommendations based on your evaluations in line with organisational requirements

e) you seek further advice from appropriate people, where necessary.

Knowledge requirements

You need to know and understand

Analytical techniques
- how to assess the advantages and disadvantages of alternative courses of action
- how to assess the applicability of technological advances in the field of energy management

Communication
- the principles and processes of effective communication and how to apply them
- how to present advice to individuals and teams

Energy efficiency
- the range of energy efficiency improvements which can be made
- developments in energy efficiency technology and best practice
- the range of energy sources and their features and benefits
- the range of available and relevant suppliers, tariffs and fuel costs

Organisational context
- the operational systems and practices in the organisation
- the organisational requirements for providing advice and recommendations
- how to decide when further advice is necessary and who to go to.

Evidence requirements

You must prove that you *recommend improvements to energy efficiency* to the National Standard of competence.

To do this, you must provide evidence to convince your assessor that you consistently meet **all** the performance criteria.

Your evidence must be the result of real work activities undertaken by yourself. Evidence from simulated activities is acceptable **only** for performance criterion e) in this element.

You must show evidence that you evaluate at least **two** of the following types of **advantages and disadvantages**
- safety
- cost
- reliability
- environment
- quality.

You must, however, convince your assessor that you have the necessary knowledge, understanding and skills to be able to perform competently in respect of **all** types of **advantages and disadvantages** listed above.

Provide advice and support for improving energy efficiency

Unit summary

This unit is about helping teams and individuals to become more efficient in the ways they use energy. It covers getting them involved in energy efficiency activities, helping them to identify the knowledge and skills they need and helping them to develop this knowledge and these skills.

This unit contains three elements

E8.1   *Encourage involvement in energy efficiency activities*
E8.2   *Provide advice on the competences needed to use energy efficiently*
E8.3   *Provide advice on the training needed to use energy efficiently.*

Personal competencies

In performing effectively in this unit, you will show that you

Communicating

- identify the information needs of listeners
- adopt communication styles appropriate to listeners and situations, including selecting an appropriate time and place
- use a variety of media and communication aids to reinforce points and maintain interest
- present difficult ideas and problems in a way that promotes understanding
- confirm listeners' understanding through questioning and interpretation of non-verbal signals
- encourage listeners to ask questions or rephrase statements to clarify their understanding
- modify communication in response to feedback from listeners

Influencing others

- present yourself positively to others
- create and prepare strategies for influencing others
- use a variety of means to influence others

Searching for information

- make best use of existing sources of information
- seek information from multiple sources
- challenge the validity and reliability of sources of information

Thinking and taking decisions

- identify a range of elements in and perspectives on a situation
- identify implications, consequences or causal relationships in a situation
- use your own experience and evidence from others to identify problems and understand situations
- identify patterns or meanings from events and data which are not obviously related
- build a total and valid picture from restricted or incomplete data.

Provide advice and support for
improving energy efficiency

Element E8.1

Encourage involvement in energy efficiency activities

Performance criteria

You must ensure that

a) you provide clear, relevant, sufficient and accessible information about energy efficient initiatives

b) you advise and encourage **relevant people** to help define their roles and responsibilities with regard to energy efficiency

c) you consistently enable **relevant people** to offer suggestions, ideas and views and to take an active part in improving the way the organisation manages energy

d) where it is not possible to act on a suggestion, you promptly provide clear and relevant reasons to those concerned

e) you consistently and effectively promote examples of good practice in energy efficiency within the organisation.

Knowledge requirements

You need to know and understand

Communication

- the principles and processes of effective communication and how to apply them
- the importance of giving clear feedback where suggestions are not taken up, and how to do this in a way which maintains morale

Energy efficiency

- the range of energy efficiency initiatives which may be used within the organisation
- a range of examples of good practice in energy efficiency and how to promote these within the organisation

Involvement and motivation

- the importance of getting people to take ownership of a problem and how to get them to do this
- how to enable people to come forward with suggestions, ideas and views
- how to enable people to take an active part in improving the way the organisation manages energy

Organisational context

- the structures and responsibilities within the organisation.

Evidence requirements

You must prove that you *encourage involvement in energy efficiency activities* to the National Standard of competence.

To do this, you must provide evidence to convince your assessor that you consistently meet **all** the performance criteria.

Your evidence must be the result of real work activities undertaken by yourself. Evidence from simulated activities is **not** acceptable for this element.

You must show evidence that your work in this area includes at least **two** of the following types of **relevant people**

- higher-level managers or sponsors
- colleagues working at the same level as yourself
- staff.

You must, however, convince your assessor that you have the necessary knowledge, understanding and skills to be able to perform competently in respect of **all** types of **relevant people** listed above.

Provide advice and support for
improving energy efficiency

Element E8.2

Provide advice on the competences needed to use energy efficiently

Performance criteria

You must ensure that

a) your **advice** takes account of all the knowledge and skills needed to achieve the organisation's energy plans

b) your **advice** takes full account of **resource** limitations

c) your **advice** is consistent with the organisation's policy and plans for energy usage

d) you provide **advice** in a manner and at a pace which meets the needs of those concerned

e) you give **relevant people** the opportunity to seek clarification of any areas of concern.

Knowledge requirements

You need to know and understand

Communication

- the principles and processes of effective communications and how to apply them
- the importance of providing people with the opportunity to ask questions and seek clarification and how to do this
- how to provide effective advice to relevant people in the organisation

Energy efficiency

- the range of knowledge and skills required to achieve energy management plans

Organisational context

- the organisation's energy policy, its strategy and plans for implementing this policy
- the organisation's resource limitations.

Evidence requirements

You must prove that you *provide advice on the competences needed to use energy efficiently* to the National Standard of competence.

To do this, you must provide evidence to convince your assessor that you consistently meet **all** the performance criteria.

Your evidence must be the result of real work activities undertaken by yourself. Evidence from simulated activities is **not** acceptable for this element.

You must show evidence that you take account of at least **two** of the following types of **resources**

- money
- people
- equipment
- energy
- premises
- materials.

You must show evidence that you provide **both** of the following types of **advice**

- written
- spoken.

You must also show evidence that your work in this area includes at least **two** of the following types of **relevant people**

- higher-level managers or sponsors
- colleagues working at the same level as yourself
- staff.

You must, however, convince your assessor that you have the necessary knowledge, understanding and skills to be able to perform competently in respect of **all** types of **resources** and **relevant people** listed above.

Provide advice and support for
improving energy efficiency

Element E8.3

Provide advice on the training needed to use energy efficiently

Performance criteria

You must ensure that

a) you give **relevant people** effective opportunities to identify the knowledge and skills they need to use energy efficiently

b) you help **relevant people** identify suitable opportunities to develop their knowledge and skills in the efficient use of energy

c) the **advice** you give is sufficient to be able to plan appropriate **training and development activities**

d) you enable **relevant people** to give useful feedback on **training and development activities** and to recommend how these activities can be improved

e) where **training and development activities** prove to be unsuitable or ineffective, you recommend suitable alternatives for the future.

Knowledge requirements

You need to know and understand

Communication
- the principles and processes of effective communication and how to apply them

Energy efficiency
- the range of knowledge and skills required to use energy efficiently
- the range of opportunities available for developing knowledge and skills in energy efficiency

Training and development
- how to identify the knowledge and skills individuals require
- how to plan training and development activities
- how to encourage people to give feedback on the training and development they have received
- how to assess whether training and development has been suitable and effective or not.

Evidence requirements

You must prove that you *provide advice on the training needed to use energy efficiently* to the National Standard of competence.

To do this, you must provide evidence to convince your assessor that you consistently meet **all** the performance criteria.

Your evidence must be the result of real work activities undertaken by yourself. Evidence from simulated activities is acceptable **only** for performance criterion e) in this element.

You must show evidence that your work in this area includes at least **two** of the following types of **relevant people**
- higher-level managers or sponsors
- colleagues working at the same level as yourself
- staff.

You must show evidence that you provide **both** of the following types of **advice**
- written
- spoken.

You must also show evidence that you use **two** of the following types of **training and development activities**
- specially allocated work activities
- formal training
- informal development activities.

You must, however, convince your assessor that you have the necessary knowledge, understanding and skills to be able to perform competently in respect of **all** types of **relevant people** and **training and development activities** listed above.

Provide advice and support for the development and implementation of quality systems

Unit summary

This unit is about helping organisations to develop and manage the systems they require to assure quality. It covers the support you give in evaluating current working environments and processes, and in developing plans to improve quality systems. It also covers your help in developing performance measuring systems and collecting and analysing information about the organisation's quality performance.

This unit contains four elements

F5.1 *Provide advice and support for the assessment of processes and working environments*

F5.2 *Provide advice and support for the development of plans to improve quality systems*

F5.3 *Provide advice and support for the development of measurement systems*

F5.4 *Provide advice and support for the collection, analysis and documentation of information.*

Personal competencies

In performing effectively in this unit, you will show that you

Communicating
- listen actively, ask questions, clarify points and rephrase others' statements to check mutual understanding
- identify the information needs of listeners
- adopt communication styles appropriate to listeners and situations, including selecting an appropriate time and place
- use a variety of media and communication aids to reinforce points and maintain interest
- present difficult ideas and problems in ways that promote understanding
- confirm listeners' understanding through questioning and interpretation of non-verbal signals
- encourage listeners to ask questions or rephrase statements to clarify their understanding

Influencing others
- present yourself positively to others
- create and prepare strategies for influencing others
- use a variety of means to influence others

Searching for information
- seek information from multiple sources
- challenge the validity and reliability of sources of information

Thinking and taking decisions
- break processes down into tasks and activities
- identify a range of elements in and perspectives on a situation
- identify implications, consequences or causal relationships in a situation
- use a range of ideas to explain the actions, needs and motives of others
- use your own experience and evidence from others to identify problems and understand situations
- take decisions which are realistic for the situation.

Provide advice and support
for the development and
implementation of quality
systems

Element F5.1

Provide advice and support for the assessment of processes and working environments

Performance criteria

You must ensure that

a) you give **relevant people** accurate
   information about the potential impact
   of work processes and **working
   environments** on meeting quality
   requirements

b) you encourage the organisation to
   develop and maintain processes, control
   systems and **working environments**
   which are appropriate for the activities
   undertaken and the people involved

c) you encourage the organisation to
   assess and improve processes and
   working environments to meet and
   improve quality standards

d) you encourage the organisation to keep
   the necessary **records** relating to
   processes and **working environments**
   and to make these available to
   authorised people when required

e) you accurately identify and advise on all
   legal requirements which affect the
   quality of products, services and
   processes.

Knowledge requirements

You need to know and understand

Communication
- the principles and processes of effective communication and how to apply them.

Legal requirements
- the principal legal requirements affecting the quality of products, services and quality.

Organisational context
- the organisation's structure and the responsibilities of people within it
- the work processes, control systems and working environments within the organisation and how to ensure these are appropriate
- the resources available and how these are used
- the records relating to processes and working environments which need to be kept
- the people who are authorised to see records relating to processes and working environments.

Quality management
- the potential impact of processes and working environments on meeting quality requirements
- the range of systems of control and how to develop appropriate systems
- the quality standards to which the organisation is working.

Evidence requirements

You must prove that you *provide advice and support for the assessment of processes and working environments* to the National Standard of competence.

To do this, you must provide evidence to convince your assessor that you consistently meet **all** the performance criteria.

Your evidence must be the result of real work activities undertaken by yourself. Evidence from simulated activities is **not** acceptable for this element.

You must show evidence that your work in this area involves at least **two** of the following types of **relevant people**
- higher-level managers or sponsors
- colleagues working at the same level as yourself
- team members
- customers
- suppliers.

You must show evidence that you consider **all** of the following aspects of **working environments**
- premises and workplace
- plant and process machinery
- materials
- operational procedures.

You must also show evidence that you help the organisation keep at least **two** of the following types of **records**
- to meet statutory requirements
- to meet non-statutory requirements
- to meet the requirements of the quality system.

You must, however, convince your assessor that you have the necessary knowledge, understanding and skills to be able to perform competently in respect of **all** types of **relevant people** and **records**, listed above.

UNIT F5

Provide advice and support for the development and implementation of quality systems

Element F5.2

Provide advice and support for the development of plans to improve quality systems

Performance criteria

You must ensure that

a) you accurately assess the organisation's ability to understand and achieve relevant quality standards and specifications

b) you give **relevant people** the necessary information and support to develop quality systems and documentation, including the definition of quality responsibilities

c) you enable **relevant people** to identify the organisation's current quality specifications and the process for developing them

d) you give **relevant people** the necessary support to develop implementation plans which include roles, responsibilities and realistic schedules

e) you give **relevant people** the necessary support to develop post-implementation monitoring procedures

f) you enable **relevant people** to agree implementation plans and post-implementation monitoring schedules with those responsible

g) you encourage **relevant people** to give their active support for quality systems.

Knowledge requirements

You need to know and understand

Communication
- the principles and processes of effective communication and how to apply them.

Involvement and motivation
- how to encourage people to give their active support for quality systems.

Monitoring and evaluation
- the principal types of monitoring procedures and how to develop them.

Organisational context
- the culture of the organisation and its level of openness to adopting quality systems
- the organisation's structure and the responsibilities of people within it
- the organisation's current quality specifications and how they were developed.

Planning
- the importance of implementation plans and how to develop them
- how to estimate realistic time schedules.

Providing support
- how to help people to present, negotiate and agree plans and monitoring procedures.

Quality management
- the range of quality standards and specifications relevant to the organisation
- how to assess the type of quality standards and specifications appropriate for the organisation
- how to develop quality systems and specifications
- how to define quality responsibilities.

Evidence requirements

You must prove that you *provide advice and support for the development of plans to improve quality systems* to the National Standard of competence.

To do this, you must provide evidence to convince your assessor that you consistently meet **all** the performance criteria.

Your evidence must be the result of real work activities undertaken by yourself. Evidence from simulated activities is **not** acceptable for this element.

You must show evidence that you give support to at least **two** of the following types of **relevant people**
- higher-level managers or sponsors
- colleagues working at the same level as yourself
- team members
- customers
- suppliers.

You must, however, convince your assessor that you have the necessary knowledge, understanding and skills to be able to perform competently in respect of **all** types of **relevant people**, listed above.

UNIT F5

Provide advice and support for the development and implementation of quality systems

Element F5.3

Provide advice and support for the development of measurement systems

Performance criteria

You must ensure that

a) you enable **relevant people** to identify the organisation's quality standards and current methods for measuring performance

b) you give **relevant people** the necessary information, advice, opportunities and encouragement to evaluate the effectiveness of the organisation's current performance measures

c) you enable **relevant people** to use performance measures and quality tools and techniques, and to incorporate them into the system design

d) you encourage **relevant people** to evaluate reports from auditors and other sources and use these in system design

e) you give **relevant people** the necessary information, advice and encouragement to develop clear and concise criteria for system design and use

f) you enable **relevant people** to design and introduce systems in ways which encourage participation

g) you enable **relevant people** to collect regular and timely information on how well the system meets the criteria, and make any necessary improvements

h) you give information and advice in a manner, and at a level and pace appropriate to the needs of the recipients.

Knowledge requirements

You need to know and understand

Analytical techniques
- how to evaluate the effectiveness of current performance measures.

Communication
- the principles and processes of effective communication and how to apply them
- how to assess the information needs of recipients and modify the content and style of your presentation accordingly.

Involvement and motivation
- how to encourage participation in the design, introduction and use of measurement systems.

Monitoring and evaluation
- how to develop clear and concise criteria.

Organisational context
- the organisation's structure and the responsibilities of people within it
- the organisation's quality standards and current methods for measuring performance.

Quality management
- the range of performance measures, quality tools and techniques which could be used
- how to design performance measurement systems
- reports from auditors and other sources and how to interpret them
- sources of reports on performance measurement systems
- the frequency with which information should be collected from the measurement systems.

Evidence requirements

You must prove that you *provide advice and support for the development of measurement systems* to the National Standard of competence.

To do this, you must provide evidence to convince your assessor that you consistently meet **all** the performance criteria.

Your evidence must be the result of real work activities undertaken by yourself. Evidence from simulated activities is **not** acceptable for this element.

You must show evidence that you give support to at least **two** of the following types of **relevant people**
- higher-level managers or sponsors
- colleagues working at the same level as yourself
- team members
- customers
- suppliers.

You must, however, convince your assessor that you have the necessary knowledge, understanding and skills to be able to perform competently in respect of **all** types of **relevant people**, listed above.

Provide advice and support
for the development and
implementation of quality
systems

Element F5.4

Provide advice and support for the collection, analysis and documentation of information

Performance criteria

You must ensure that

a) you agree with **relevant people** the nature and extent of the **support** they need

b) you give **relevant people** clear and justifiable advice on how to use quality management **tools and techniques** in their work

c) you give **support** to ensure that any necessary documentation relating to quality management is made available within agreed timescales

d) you give **support** in a manner which is appropriate to the people concerned and demonstrates respect for the individual

e) you encourage **relevant people** to report on progress with collecting, analysing and interpreting information and to ask for further help when needed.

Knowledge requirements

You need to know and understand

Communication
- the principles and processes of effective communication
- how to provide clear and relevant advice.

Information handling
- the principles of confidentiality and respect for the individual and how to apply them.

Organisational context
- the organisation's requirements for documentation relating to quality management.

Providing support
- how to establish the amount of support individuals and teams need
- how to provide support in an appropriate manner
- how to encourage feedback and requests for help when required.

Quality management
- the range of quality management tools and techniques
- the techniques of data collection, analysis and recording.

Evidence requirements

You must prove that you *provide advice and support for the collection, analysis and documentation of information* to the National Standard of competence.

To do this, you must provide evidence to convince your assessor that you consistently meet **all** the performance criteria.

Your evidence must be the result of real work activities undertaken by yourself. Evidence from simulated activities is **not** acceptable for this element.

You must show evidence that you give support to at least **two** of the following types of **relevant people**
- higher-level managers or sponsors
- colleagues working at the same level as yourself
- team members
- customers
- suppliers.

You must show evidence that you provide at least **two** of the following types of **support**
- provision of information and advice
- accessing expertise
- training people
- working with people on particular objectives or activities.

You must also show evidence that you give advice on the use of at least **three** of the following types of **tools and techniques**
- quality planning
- defining criteria
- evaluating tools
- controlling plans
- monitoring cost of quality.

You must, however, convince your assessor that you have the necessary knowledge, understanding and skills to be able to perform competently in respect of **all** types of **relevant people**, **support** and **tools and techniques**, listed above.

Carry out quality audits

Unit summary

This unit is about assessing the extent to which individuals and teams either within your organisation or in other organisations comply with agreed quality systems and procedures. It covers carrying out audits and reporting the results.

This unit contains two elements

F7.1 *Audit compliance with quality systems*
F7.2 *Follow up quality audits.*

Personal competencies

In performing effectively in this unit, you will show that you

Communicating
- adopt communication styles appropriate to listeners and situations, including selecting an appropriate time and place
- confirm listeners' understanding through questioning and interpretation of non-verbal signals
- encourage listeners to ask questions or rephrase statements to clarify their understanding

Influencing others
- present yourself positively to others

Searching for information
- seek information from multiple sources
- challenge the validity and reliability of sources of information
- push for concrete information in an ambiguous situation

Thinking and taking decisions
- break processes down into tasks and activities
- identify a range of elements in and perspectives on a situation
- identify implications, consequences or causal relationships in a situation
- use your own experience and evidence from others to identify problems and understand situations
- take decisions which are realistic for the situation.

Carry out quality audits

Element F7.1

Audit compliance with quality systems

Performance criteria

You must ensure that

a) you carry out quality audits according to an agreed plan and schedule

b) you give **auditees** the required period of notice of your intention to audit

c) you clearly confirm the responsibilities of **auditees** and the procedures which apply to their work

d) your audit investigation is sufficiently detailed to reveal any discrepancies

e) for each discrepancy found, you agree with **auditees** appropriate corrective action and the date by which it should be carried out

f) you seek advice from **relevant people** if you cannot agree a discrepancy or corrective action with **auditees**

g) you conduct audits in a way which enhances the confidence and commitment to quality of **auditees**

h) you complete records of the quality audit in accordance with agreed procedures.

Knowledge requirements

You need to know and understand

Analytical techniques
- how to evaluate actual practice against procedures in order to identify discrepancies.

Communication
- the principles and processes of effective communication and how to apply them.

Information handling
- methods of seeking out information and how to apply them.

Involvement and motivation
- how to enhance the confidence and commitment of those being audited.

Organisational context
- the organisation's quality policies and procedures
- the organisation's plan and schedule for carrying out quality audits
- the organisation's structure and the responsibilities of people within it
- the people to turn to for advice on quality auditing issues
- the records of the quality audit that are required.

Quality management
- the period of notice of intention to audit required
- the procedures which apply to different people
- the principles of quality auditing and how to conduct an audit investigation
- how to identify appropriate corrective action and agree a reasonable date for it to be carried out.

Evidence requirements

You must prove that you *audit compliance with quality systems* to the National Standard of competence.

To do this, you must provide evidence to convince your assessor that you consistently meet **all** the performance criteria.

Your evidence must be the result of real work activities undertaken by yourself. Evidence from simulated activities is acceptable **only** for performance criterion f) in this element.

You must show evidence that you audit **one** of the following types of **auditees**
- individuals and teams within your organisation
- individuals and teams in other organisations.

You must also show evidence that you seek advice from **one** of the following types of **relevant people**
- higher-level managers or sponsors
- colleagues working at the same level as yourself
- quality specialists.

You must, however, convince your assessor that you have the necessary knowledge, understanding and skills to be able to perform competently in respect of **all** types of **auditees** and **relevant people**, listed above.

Carry out quality audits

Element F7.2

Follow up quality audits

Performance criteria

You must ensure that

a) you make your quality audit reports available to authorised people in accordance with the organisation's procedures

b) you promptly bring to the attention of **relevant people** any discrepancies which hold serious or immediate risks for the organisation

c) you check with **auditees** that corrective action has been carried out by the agreed dates

d) you report persistent problems in achieving compliance with quality systems to **relevant people**

e) you make appropriate recommendations for improvements to procedures to **relevant people**.

Knowledge requirements

You need to know and understand

Communication

- the principles and processes of effective communication and how to apply them
- how to make recommendations for improvements.

Organisational context

- the organisation's quality policies and procedures
- the organisation's plan and schedule for carrying out quality audits
- the organisation's structure and the responsibilities of people within it
- the people who are authorised to see quality audit reports.

Quality management

- the principles of quality auditing and how to conduct an audit investigation
- how to evaluate the risks which discrepancies may hold for the organisation
- the corrective action and dates agreed with auditees
- reports from auditors and how to interpret them.

Evidence requirements

You must prove that you *follow up quality audits* to the National Standard of competence.

To do this, you must provide evidence to convince your assessor that you consistently meet **all** the performance criteria.

Your evidence must be the result of real work activities undertaken by yourself. Evidence from simulated activities is acceptable **only** for performance criterion d) in this element.

You must show evidence that you make recommendations for improvements to **one** of the following types of **relevant people**

- higher-level managers or sponsors
- colleagues working at the same level as yourself
- quality specialists.

You must also show evidence that you check that corrective action has been carried out by **one** of the following types of **auditees**

- individuals and teams within your organisation
- individuals and teams in other organisations.

You must, however, convince your assessor that you have the necessary knowledge, understanding and skills to be able to perform competently in respect of **all** types of **relevant people** and **auditees**, listed above.

Index

Note: page references for major topics of units
are shown in **bold**

A

acting assertively
  information for action 35
  personnel selection 45
  poor performance in teams 69, 71
  relationships, effective working 27
  self-management 21
  teams and individuals 51, 61
advantages of energy efficiency 78, 79
advice and support
  for energy efficiency improvement **80–7**
    training 86–7
  and information to others 38–9
  quality systems development and
    implementation **88–97**
analytical techniques
  energy efficiency 79
  information for action 37
  maintaining activities 11, 13
  quality audits 101
  quality systems 95
  resources, efficient use of 17
approved centre 2
assertive action *see* acting assertively *see also*
  personal competencies
assessment
  of people against development objectives 58–9
  personnel 59, 64, 65
  self-management 22, 23
  work of teams and individuals 64–5
see also monitoring
assessor 2–3
audits, quality **98–103**
authorised people
  development of teams and individuals 52, 53,
    54, 55
  personnel selection 48

B

behaving ethically 45, 69
benefits of energy efficiency 78, 79
building teams 51
  information for action 35
  leadership 61
  maintaining activities 7

poor performance 69
relationships, effective working 27

C

colleagues and team members
  energy efficiency 83, 85, 87
  information for action 39
  maintaining activities 9, 11, 13
  poor performance in teams 70–1
  problems 32–3, 70–1
  quality audits 101, 103
  quality systems 91, 93, 95, 97
  relationships, effective working 27, 28–9, 32–3
  resources, efficient use of 17, 19
  self-management 23
  see also teams
communicating *see* personal competencies
communication *see also* knowledge requirements
  advice and support 81, 83, 85, 87
  energy efficiency improvement 75, 77, 79
  information for action 35, 39, 41
  maintaining activities 7, 9, 11, 13
  personnel selection 45, 47, 49
  poor performance in teams 69
  quality audits 101, 103
  quality systems 89, 91, 93, 95, 97
  relationships, effective working 27, 29, 31
  resources, efficient use of 15, 17, 19
  self-management 21, 23
  teams and individuals
    development 51, 53
    leadership 61, 63, 65, 67
conflict minimisation in teams 32–3
constraints
  organisational 62, 63
  work 46, 47
consultation meeting 41
continuous improvement 3
  maintaining activities 13
  teams and individuals
    development 53, 55, 57
    leadership 63, 65, 67
contribution to development activities 56–7
control of resources 18–19
corrective action and resource use 18, 19
customers/customer relations
  maintaining activities 8, 9
  quality systems 91, 93, 95, 97

D

decisions, taking *see* thinking
development
  quality systems **88–97**
  teams and individuals **50–9**
  skills 22–3
  see also building teams; training and
    development
disciplinary and grievance procedures 72–3

E

effective working relationships **26–33**
efficiency in resource use **14–19**
energy efficiency/energy management
  advice and support for **80–7**
  identification **74–9**
environment/environmental management
  impact on 18, 77
  working 10–11
ethical behaviour 45, 69
evaluation *see* monitoring
evidence requirements 1

F

feedback on work of teams and individuals 66–7
focusing on results
  and maintaining activities 7
  poor performance in teams 69
  resources, efficient use of 15
  self-management 21
forms of team feedback 66, 67

G

goals *see* objectives
grievance procedures 72–3

H

health and safety
  maintaining 10–11
  requirements 9

I

identification of development needs 52–3
improvement
  through skills development 22–3
  to work activities, recommending 12–13

  see also continuous improvement; energy
    efficiency
information management
  for action **34–41**
  and advice to others 38–9
  disciplinary and grievance procedures 72, 73
  energy efficiency 81
  gathering 36–7
  given at meeting 41
  handling
    information for action 37, 39
    personnel selection 47, 49
    poor performance in teams 71, 73
    quality audits 101
    quality systems 97
    relationships, effective working 29, 33
    self-management 25
    teams and individuals 53, 59, 65, 67
  personnel assessment 64, 65
  qualitative and quantitative 37, 65
  quality audits 99
  quality systems 89
  see also searching for information
involvement and motivation
  energy efficiency 77, 82–3
  maintaining activities 9
  quality audits 101
  quality systems 93, 95
  resources, efficient use of 17, 19
  teams and individuals
    development 53, 55, 59
    leadership 63, 65, 67

K

key roles 1–2
knowledge requirements 1
  analytical techniques 11, 13, 17, 37, 79, 95, 101
  communication 9, 11, 13, 17, 19, 23, 29, 31,
    39, 41, 47, 49, 53, 63, 65, 67, 71, 77, 79, 83,
    85, 87, 91, 93, 95, 97, 101, 103
  continuous improvement 13, 53, 57, 63, 65, 67
  customer relations 9
  disciplinary and grievance procedures 73
  energy efficiency 77, 79, 83, 85, 87
  environmental management 77
  health and safety 11
  information handling 25, 29, 33, 37, 39, 47,
    49, 53, 59, 65, 67, 71, 73, 97, 101

involvement and motivation 9, 17, 19, 53, 55,
59, 63, 65, 67, 77, 83, 93, 95, 101
leadership styles 41
legal requirements 47, 49, 73, 91
management competence 23
meetings 41
monitoring and evaluation 9, 25, 65, 71, 93, 95
organisational context 9, 11, 13, 17, 19, 23,
29, 31, 33, 37, 39, 41, 47, 49, 53, 55, 59, 63,
73, 77, 79, 83, 85, 91, 93, 95, 97, 101, 103
planning 9, 25, 63, 93
providing support 29, 71, 93, 97
quality management 91, 93, 95, 97, 101, 103
recruitment and selection 47, 49
resource management 17, 19
time management 25
training and development 23, 53, 55, 57, 59, 87
working relationships 29, 31, 33, 63, 71, 73
workplace organisation 11

L

leadership
styles 41
of teams and individuals **60–7**
legal requirements
personnel selection 47, 49
poor performance in teams 73
quality systems 91

M

maintaining activities to meet requirements **6–13**
management competence 23 ; see also
knowledge requirements
managing self **20–5**, 27
mandatory units 6–41
meetings, holding 40–1
monitoring and evaluation
leadership of teams and individuals 65
maintaining activities 9
poor performance in teams 71
quality systems 93, 95
self-management 25
see also assessment
motivation see involvement and motivation

N

National Vocational Qualifications (NVQ) 1, 2–3
negative feedback 67

O

objectives
development, assessment of people against
58–9
leading team and individual work to achieve
60–7
self-management 23
team 53
time management to meet own 24–5
work 46, 47
opportunities to improve energy efficiency 76–7
optional units 43–103

P

performance criteria 1
personal competencies 1
acting assertively 21, 27, 35, 45, 51, 61, 69,
behaving ethically 45, 69,
building teams 7, 27, 35, 51, 61, 69,
communicating 7, 15, 21, 27, 35, 45, 51, 61,
69, 75, 81, 89, 99,
focusing on results 7, 15, 21, 69,
influencing others 35, 45, 75, 81, 89, 99,
managing self 21, 27,
searching for information 35, 45, 75, 81, 89, 99,
thinking and taking decisions 7, 15, 21, 27, 35,
45, 51, 61, 75, 81, 89, 99,
personnel selection **44–9**
planning
maintaining activities 9
quality systems 93
self-management 25
teams and individuals
development 54–5
leadership 62–3
poor performance in teams **68–73**
positive feedback 67
problems of team members 32–3, 70–1
productive working conditions
maintaining 10–11
proposals and relationships, working 30, 31
purposes
of meetings 40, 41
of personnel assessment 59, 64, 65

Q

qualitative information 37, 65

quality/quality management
  audits **98–103**
  requirements 9
  resources 18
  systems development and implementation
    88–97
quantitative information 37, 65
quantity requirements 9

R

recommendations
  energy efficiency improvement 78–9
  improvements to work activities 12–13
recommendations for use of resources 16–17
records, keeping 18, 90, 91
recruitment 47, 49; *see also* personnel selection
relationships *see* working relationships
requirements 9
  maintaining activities to meet **6–13**
  personnel, identifying 46–7
  see also legal
resources/resource management
  efficient use of **14–19**
  types of 77, 85
  see also energy
results *see* focusing on results

S

safety *see* health and safety
Scottish Vocational Qualifications (SVQ) 1, 2–3
searching for information
  energy efficiency 75, 81
  information for action 35, 36–7
  personnel selection 45
  quality audits 99
  quality systems 89
self-management **20–5**, 27
skills development 22–3
support
  of colleagues and team members 28–9
  of manager 30–1
  quality systems 93, 97
  relationships, effective working 29
  team members with problems 32–3, 71
  see also advice and support
systems and procedures and information
  gathering 36–7

T

teams
  development **50–9**
  leadership **60–7**
  poor performance **68–73**
  see also building teams; colleagues and team
    members
thinking and taking decisions
  energy efficiency 75, 81
  information for action 35, 41
  and maintaining activities 7
  personnel selection 45
  quality audits 99
  quality systems 89
  relationships, effective working 27
  resources, efficient use of 15
  self-management 21
  teams and individuals 51, 61
time management to meet own objectives 24–5
tools and techniques 97
training and development
  energy efficiency 86–7
  self-management 23
  teams and individuals 53, 55, 57
  see also development
trust, gaining
  of colleagues and team members 28–9
  of manager 30–1

U

units of competence 1

W

working conditions, healthy, safe and productive
  10–11
working relationships, effective **26–33**
  leadership of teams and individuals 63
  poor performance in teams 71, 72
workplace organisation 11